DOG IN THE TUB

AN EARLY READER SERIES

READER 1

A Map 1
The Sun 2
Dog in the Tub 5
Dad 6
Wet 7
Getting Dressed to Go Out in the Rain 9
Sis 10
My Bible 11
What Is in the Pot? 12
My Rag Doll 14
Tom 15
A Very Big Mess! 17
Our Pet 19
Jesus 20
Run 21
Little Red Fox 23
Bzz! 24
Mom 25
The Big Fat Hen 27
Tim Kicks 28
Ball Fun 29
Fast Jim 31
Little Black Ants 33
Bug 35

Authors:
Annie Brown
Alpha Omega Staff

804 N. 2nd Ave. E.
Rock Rapids, IA 51246-1759

Instant Words

1.	the	he	go	who
2.	a	I	see	an
3.	is	they	then	their
4.	you	one	us	she
5.	to	good	no	new
6.	and	me	him	said
7.	we	about	by	did
8.	that	had	was	boy
9.	in	if	come	three
10.	not	some	get	down
11.	for	up	or	work
12.	at	her	two	put
13.	with	do	man	were
14.	it	when	little	before
15.	on	so	has	just
16.	can	my	them	long

17.	will	very	how	here
18.	are	all	like	other
19.	of	would	our	old
20.	this	any	what	take
21.	your	been	know	cat
22.	as	out	make	again
23.	but	there	which	give
24.	be	from	much	after
25.	have	day	his	many
26.	fall	love	ball	bzz
27.	Bible	to	my	by

A Map

Look! There is a map.
It is a flat map.
I will pick up the map.
It will tell me where to go.

The Sun

The sun is fun.
I will sit in the sun.

I will sit on a mat.
The sun is not fun.

The sun is hot!
I will get a fan.

I will get a hat.
Now the sun is fun.

Dog in the Tub

"This dog needs a bath," said Jill.

"Yes, he does!" said Bill.

"Let's put the dog in the tub," said Jill.

"I will help you pick him up," said Bill.

Up, up, up

we go

and

in, in, in

he goes.

Kerplop!

Can you guess

who got wet?

Dad

I will run to Dad.
I will hug Dad.
I fit in his hug.

Wet

Jill will get wet!
Bill will get wet!
The fat cat and Jan will not get wet.

Getting Dressed to Go Out in the Rain

Get your green jacket and
zip it up.

Get your blue hat and
put it on your head.

Get your big red umbrella.

Put it up and over your head,
then out
the door
you can go.

Sis

Sis is sad.
Sis did not get to toss the ball.
I will toss the ball to Sis.
Sis will not be sad.

My Bible

I have a red Bible.
I will sit on my mat.
I will not let my Bible fall.
It will tell of God.

What Is in the Pot?

What is in the pot?
I see it is not hot.
So, what is in the pot?

What is in the cup?
I see it is not a pup.
So, what is in the cup?

What is in the sack?
I see it is not black.
So, what is in the sack?

What is in the box?
I see it is not a fox.
So, what is in the box?

#1

My Rag Doll

Mom can make me a doll.
She will get bits of cloth and rags.
My doll will have a red dress.
My doll will have yellow socks.
My doll will have long black hair.

I will give my doll a name.
Her name will be Sam.
She will sit on my bed.
Sam will be my rag doll.

Tom

Tom will huff and puff.
He will dig and pull.
He will fix the hill.

A Very Big Mess!

Oh, what a mess mud can be.

Dig in it.

Sit in it.

Kick in it.

Oh, what a mess mud can be.

Plop in it.

Drop in it.

Flop in it.

Oh, what a mess mud can be.

Run in it.

Jump in it.

Have fun in it.

Oh, what a mess mud can be.

Yes, yes!
A very big mess!

Our Pet

We got a pet from a man named Dan.
He got it from the vet.
It is a she and not a he.
She is a very good pet.

We gave her a name.
It's Pinky Sue.
Call her like this, "P i n k y
S u u u u u u u e!"
She'll come running to you.

Our pet is not a dog.
Our pet is not a cat.
Maybe you can guess our pet.
If I told you she was pink and fat.

Jesus

Jesus will hug.
Jesus will tell of God.
Jesus is love.
Jesus is the Son of God.

Run

Ron and Deb will run.
Don and John will run.
Bob and Tom will run.
Jill and Kim will run.
Will Ron fall?

Little Red Fox

A little red fox ran up the hill.
Up the very big hill.

He got to the top as the sun went down.
Then up and over the hill he went.
The little red fox was gone.

I wonder where the little red fox went.
I wonder what he sees.
Did he go home to his den?
Did he see his Mom and Dad?
I want to know, I want to know.

I hope the little red fox comes back.
Then I can ask of him:
Where is it you go?
What do you see over the hill?
I want to know, I want to know.
Won't you tell me please?

Bzz!

Bzz, Bzz!
Bzz, Bzz, Bzz!
It is a bug!

Run, Run, Run!
This bug will not hug!

Mom

Mom is not well.
We will not sit.
We will jog with the dog.
We will pick up this mess.
Mom will get well.

The Big Fat Hen

Matt sees the big fat hen.
Jan sees the big fat hen.
Tom and Tim see the big fat hen.

The man sees the big fat hen.
The dog and cat see the big fat hen.
The pig sees the big fat hen.

The big fat hen is by the pen.
The big fat hen sits on her nest.
"Cluck, cluck!" says the big fat hen.

The big fat hen sees Matt, Jan, Tom,
and Tim.
The big fat hen sees the man, the dog,
and the cat.
But she does not see the pig.

Tim Kicks

Tim is not big.
But Tim can kick.
He can kick the ball.
Can he kick the ball to Tom?
Yes! He can!

Ball Fun

Tom has the ball.
Tom will run.
Bob will run.
Bob will get the ball!

Fast Jim

Jim will get to bat.
Don will toss the ball to Jim.
Jim will hit the ball and run.
He is fast.
Jim will run and run.

Don will get the ball that Jim hit.
He will not miss.
Don will toss the ball to Pat.
Run, Jim, run!
The ball is in Pat's mitt.

The fans yell, "Hurray!" for Jim.
Jim is so glad he is fast.

Little Black Ants

Sit by the hill
when the sun
comes up.

Little black ants come out.
See them go down the path one by one.
They work and work all day.

Little black ants go back to the hill.
Back to the hill
when the sun
goes down.

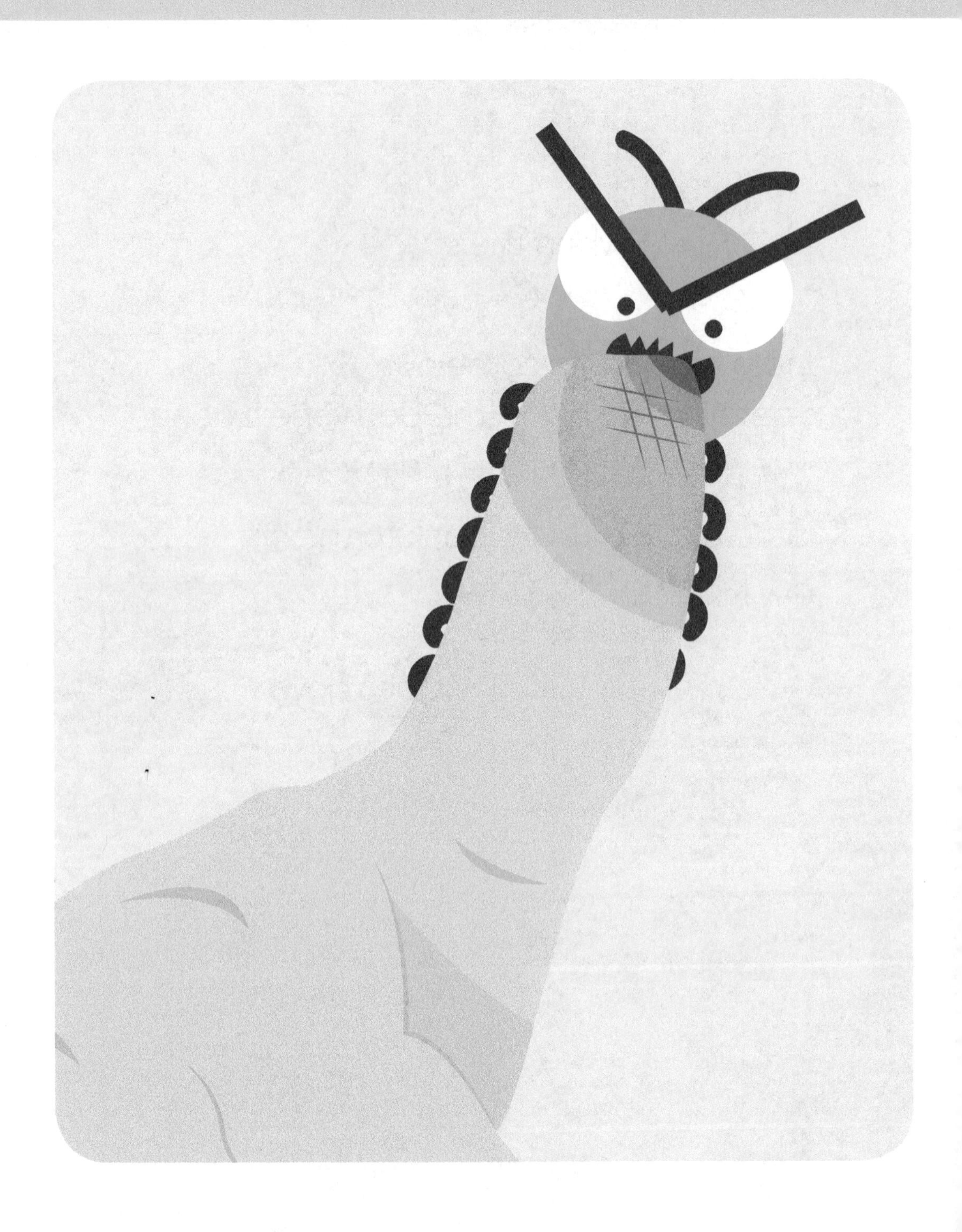

Bug

I was bit by a big bad bug.
Bug, bug, bug.
Mom had a kiss.
Dad had a hug.
Hug, hug, hug.
I did not hit the big bad bug.
Bug, bug, bug.
But Dad did.

NOTES